4 Read-Aloud Stories

BLOCKCHAIN
Tales

Storybook Companion to

the Blockchain Basics Curriculum

★ ★ ★ ★ ★

WAGMI CONSULTING GROUP
Elizabeth Sullivan

The Blockchain Odyssey

UNIT

1

THE
BLOCKCHAIN
ODYSSEY

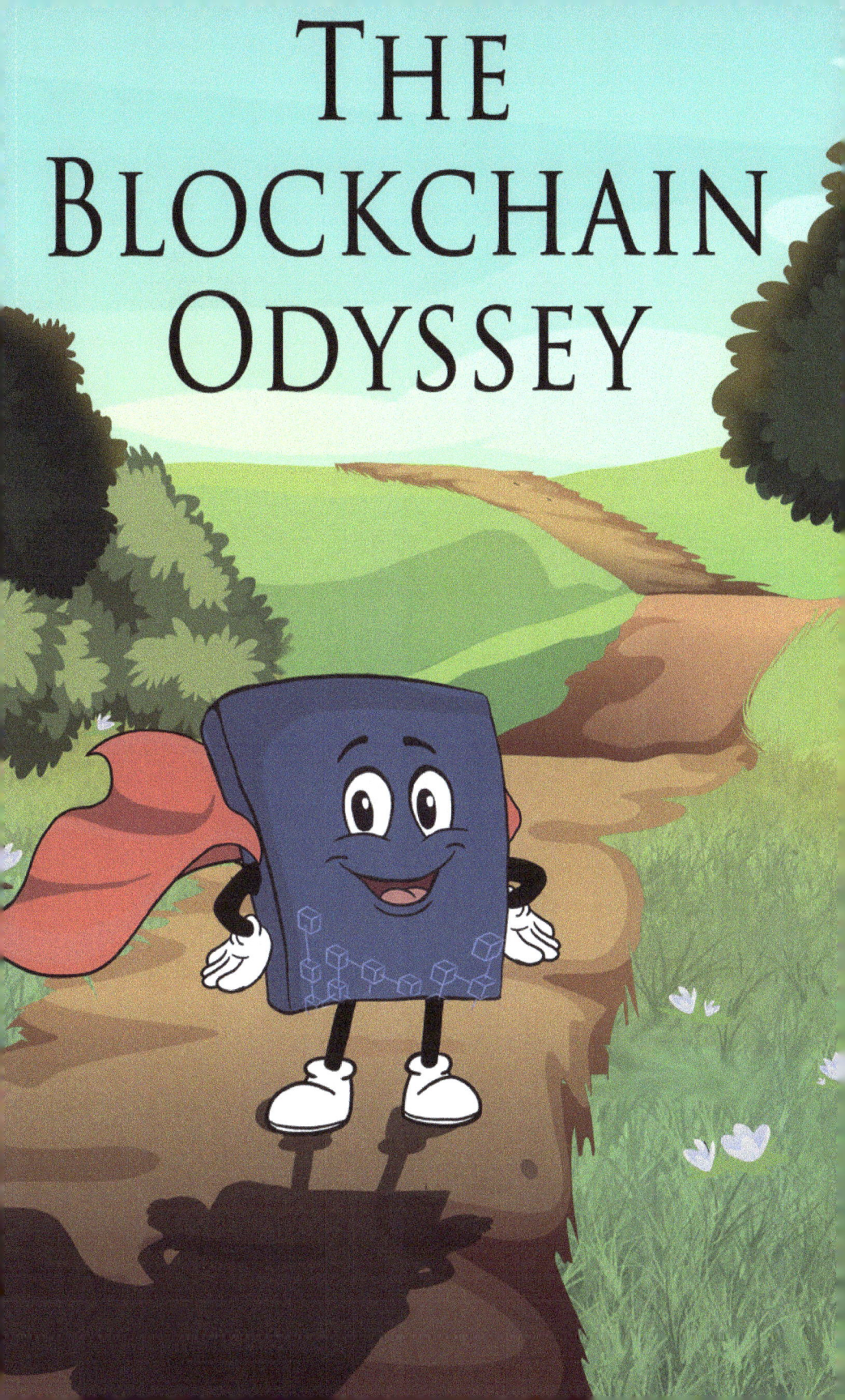

Once on a desk sat a little notebook. At first, it was just blank pages. But one day, a wise old computer expert saw it and smiled.

"I'm giving you the power of blockchain technology," he said. With that, the notebook was no longer ordinary.

He turned it into a digital notebook and gave it the name Scribblet. "You will help people keep track of important things safely," he said. Scribblet lit up. "I have a purpose now! I can't wait to use this new power!"
And with that, Scribblet set off on it's big adventure.

And with that, Scribblet set off on it's big adventure. As Scribblet traveled through the metaverse, it met new friends.

"Who are you all?" it asked.
"We're nodes," said one. "We help keep the blockchain safe and accurate. We all agree before anything is added. That's called consensus. "Scribblet beamed. "You're like superheroes! I'm glad we're on the same team."

Scribblet also discovered other notebooks.

Public Notebooks that anyone can read and write in. Private Notebooks for certain people only. And Consortium Notebooks shared between groups. Each one had its own job. Some helped share info with friends. Others kept track of deals and promises.

Scribblet learned more as it traveled such as, how to keep records safe, and how to protect digital identities. It also learned how to use smart contracts. "What are those?" someone asked. Scribblet explained, "They're digital agreements that run by themselves if the rules are met. Like renting an apartment, the contract sends the rent to the landlord automatically." Everyone was amazed. "That's so helpful!" Scribblet enjoyed helping people stay organized and honest.

Scribblet visited places like banks and hospitals. "I can help make transactions faster and more secure," Scribblet told them. "How?" they each asked.

"Through blockchain record-keeping. It creates a record no one can change. Doctors could even use it to safely store health records."

"Wow!" they said. "We need that!"

Scribblet also learned how to stay safe.
It had a blockchain wallet where people kept
digital coins like Bitcoin. To use it, they needed:
A public address to receive coins, and a private
key to access them. Scribblet used strong
passwords and something called Two-Factor
Authentication. Kind of like adding a second
lock. It also kept it's private key offline so no
one could steal it.

BLOCKCHAIN

Scribblet kept learning more about things it could do using strategies like proof of work and proof of stake. "Proof of work means solving hard puzzles to add things to the blockchain. It's called mining," Scribblet explained. "Proof of stake doesn't use puzzles. Instead, people lock up some of their coins to help confirm transactions. Both methods help keep the blockchain safe and fair." People were amazed by how many ways blockchain could help them.

Scribblet felt a sense of pride and satisfaction at being able to help people in such a meaningful way. With its help, people kept promises, tracked data, and stayed safe. "I'm glad I can be of service," said Scribblet. It had become a big part of many important places—and it wasn't done yet.

One day, Scribblet heard Nodes whisper about new adventures. "Gaming, events, even voting!" said a node. "Blockchain can help with all of them. Even helping people manage their digital identity." "Really?" Scribblet asked thoughtfully, "I'm ready. Let's keep going."

Scribblet reflected with pride. "I started as a plain notebook. Now I help so many people!" Scribblet smiled. "And there's more to do. The journey isn't over. There are still new places, new friends, and new lessons ahead.

And the Blockchain Odyssey continues...

Welcome To Nodesville

UNIT
2

Jesse was a Node who had just moved to Nodesville. It seemed like a nice place, but he was curious about how everything worked.

Thankfully, his new friend Jen was there to show him around.

"Welcome to Nodesville, Jesse!" Jen greeted him warmly.

"Thank you!" Jesse said excitedly. "Everything here seems so interesting. Can you show me around? I want to learn all about this node-life!"

"Of course!" Jen replied with a smile. "In Nodesville, each of us nodes has an important job on the blockchain. Let me introduce you to some of the others and show you how everything works."

First Jen took Jesse to the Library of Nodesville.

"Jesse, I would like you to meet Lucy, she is our digital librarian" Jen explained. "She helps keep everything in town organized."

"Hi Jesse!" Lucy greeted him warmly. "Yes, I keep a digital record of everything that happens here, so that nothing important gets lost."

"Woah! That sounds like a big responsibility!" Jesse exclaimed.

"It is," Lucy agreed. "But I share copies of these records with other librarian nodes in nearby towns. That way, if something happens to one record, we always have backups."

Jen added, "Librarian Lucy shares data so that each node has a copy to ensure everything stays accurate."

Next, Jen and Jesse walked to the town square to meet the Sheriff.

"Jesse, I'd like to introduce you to Sheriff Shane," Jen said. "he makes sure everything in Nodesville is fair."

"Howdy, Jesse!" Shane said with a friendly nod. "I check that every trade or deal is fair and honest."

"Why is that important?" Jesse asked.

"It's all about validating trust," Shane explained. "If someone tries to trade something they don't have, the system wouldn't work."

Jen added, "Before any transaction is added to the blockchain, nodes like Sheriff Shane check to make sure everything is correct."

Jen and Jesse walked up to the town hall, where they met Mayor Katie. The big building was buzzing with activity as nodes discussed new ideas.

"This is Mayor Katie," Jen said. "She makes sure everything runs smoothly by helping create the rules we all follow."

"Hello Jesse!" Mayor Katie said with a smile. "In Nodesville, we work together to agree on important decisions, like adding new rules."

"How do you do that?" Jesse asked curiously.

"That's where consensus comes in," Mayor Katie explained. "Consensus means that all of us nodes have to agree before any new information or rules are added. We discuss, compare ideas, and make sure we all have the same understanding. Once we all agree, the new rule gets added to the rulebook, and everyone follows it."

"So you all have to agree before something can change?" Jesse asked. "Yes!" Mayor Katie replied. "This way, no one can make changes on their own, and everyone can trust the system because it's fair."

Jen smiled and added, "In Nodesville, reaching consensus is what keeps our town organized and secure."

As they continued their walk, Jen and Jesse passed by Captain Carver and his team of guards, who stood watch in the tower.

"These are the Nodesville Guards," Jen said. "They protect our town's rulebook and make sure no one changes the rules without permission."

"We're always on guard," Captain Carver said proudly.

"And if something's wrong, we fix it right away!" added the other guard.

"That sounds really important. How do you know if something's wrong?" Jesse asked.

Captain Carter continued, "We check our rulebook against copies from other towns. We nodes work together to notice everything."

Jen explained further, "On the blockchain, nodes like the Guards constantly check the data. If anything seems wrong, they fix it to keep the information honest and safe."

Finally, Jen and Jesse visited the town's Contractor, who was busy building something new.

"Last but not least, this is Contractor Connor," Jen said. "He builds projects using blueprints called 'smart contracts.'"

"Hi Jesse!" Connor greeted him with a grin. "My blueprints tell me exactly what to do, step by step. Once I start, the smart contract makes sure the job is finished perfectly."

"That sounds like a cool way to build things, Connor!" Jesse said, fascinated.

"It is!" Connor agreed. "The best part is that the smart contract doesn't let me skip any steps or make mistakes. They automatically execute tasks on the blockchain when certain conditions are met. So everything happens exactly as planned."

After meeting all the nodes, Jesse felt much more confident about how everything in Nodesville worked.

"Thanks, Jen! I get it now, every node has a job that keeps the town blockchain running smoothly" Jesse said smiling.

Jen nodded. "That's right! In Nodesville we all work together. Each node is important, just like you'll be."

As they walked back through the town, Jen asked, "So, what kind of node do you think you'd want to be? Maybe you'd like to decide consensus like Mayor Katie, or perhaps you'd enjoy building things like Contractor Connor. Or, who knows, you might come up with a brand new kind of node that we haven't even imagined yet!"

Jesse thought about all the possibilities. Whatever role he chose, he knew he wanted to make a difference and was excited to find his place.

Jen smiled at him and said, "No matter what you decide, I know you'll be a great addition to Nodesville."

What Do Nodes Do?

In a blockchain, nodes keep everything running smoothly. Nodes are computers or devices connected to the blockchain network, and each one has an important job. Let's break down what nodes do and why they matter!

Storing and Sharing Information:

Every node on a blockchain holds a full copy of all the information, like records or transactions. When new information is added, it gets shared with all the nodes in the network. This means if one node loses its data or stops working, there are many other nodes that still have the correct information. This keeps the blockchain safe and reliable.

Checking Transactions:

Before a new transaction (like sending money or trading something) is added to the blockchain, nodes check to make sure everything is correct. This is called validation. The nodes confirm that the transaction follows the rules and that the person making the trade owns what they're trading. Only after the nodes say it's okay can the transaction be added. This helps keep the system honest and trustworthy.

Agreeing on New Information (Consensus):

Nodes don't work alone. They have to agree with each other before new information is added to the blockchain. This process is called consensus. Different blockchains have different ways of doing this, but the idea is the same: the nodes work together to decide what information is real and what gets added. This keeps the blockchain fair and secure because nothing can be added unless the nodes agree.

Keeping the Blockchain Safe:

Nodes also help protect the blockchain from hackers or anyone trying to change the information. If someone tries to mess with the data, the nodes compare their copies and fix any problems. This makes the blockchain very secure because no single person or computer can secretly change the information without the other nodes noticing and fixing it.

Running Smart Contracts:

Some blockchains use smart contracts, which are programs that automatically do something when certain conditions are met. For example, a smart contract might send money automatically after a job is finished. Nodes help by running these smart contracts, making sure everything happens as the rules say it should.

Why Are Nodes Important?

Nodes are the backbone of a blockchain. They store and share information, check that transactions are correct, agree on new data to add, protect the system from being hacked, and run smart contracts. Without nodes, the blockchain wouldn't be able to work. Nodes working together are what keep the blockchain safe, reliable, and strong.

In a blockchain, **every node is important** because each one helps keep the system running smoothly!

Cryptonia
Chronicles
UNIT
3

Cryptonia
CHRONICLES

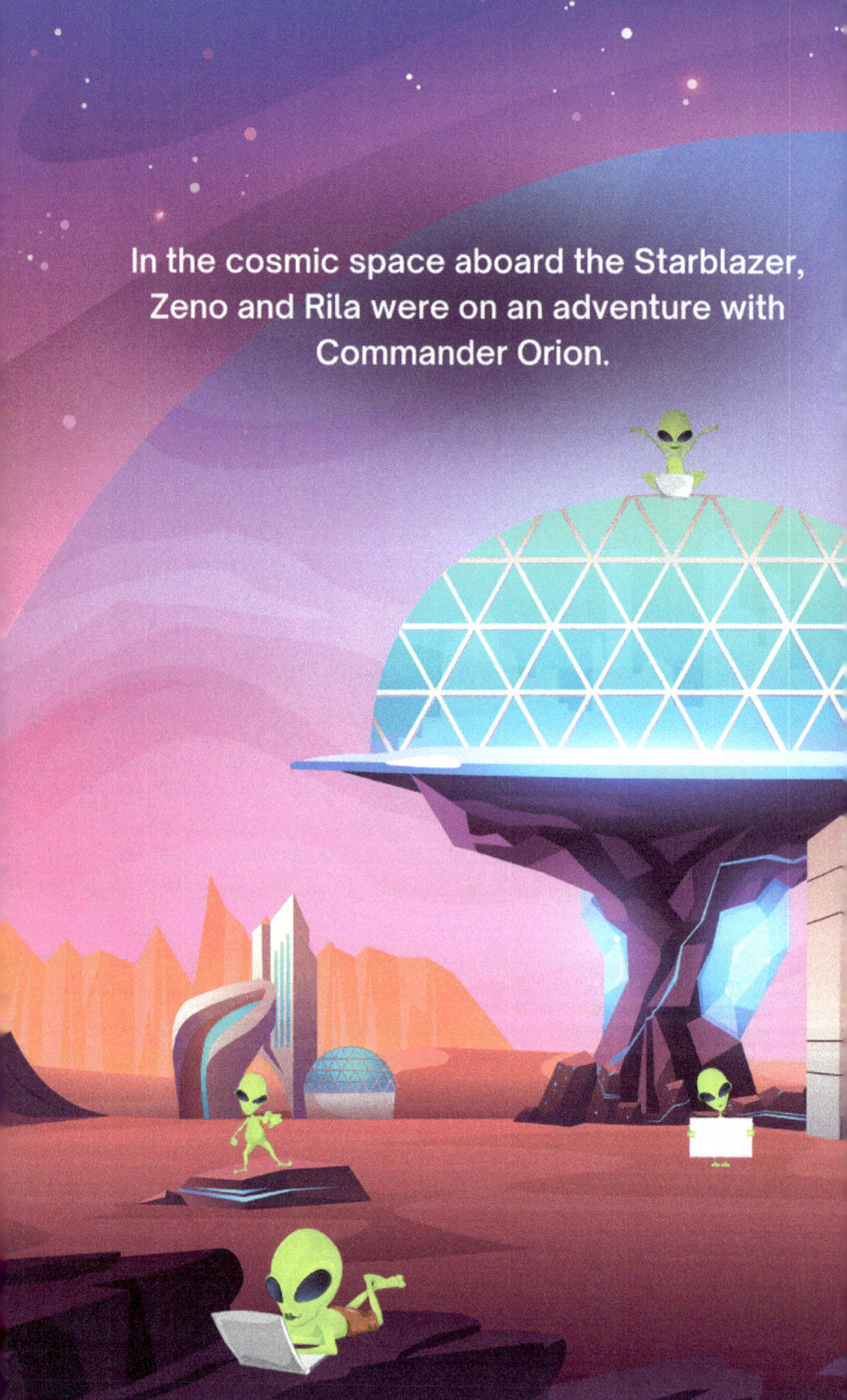

In the cosmic space aboard the Starblazer, Zeno and Rila were on an adventure with Commander Orion.

The intergalactic federation had chosen them to explore Cryptonia, a planet renowned for its use of cryptocurrency in everyday life.

"Prepare for landing!" Commander Orion declared with excitement as the planet came into view. "I can't wait to learn about their new technology and see how it powers the entire planet!"

Unlike any other place, Cryptonia didn't have coins or paper money; instead, its residents used digital money to pay for activities and experiences across the planet.

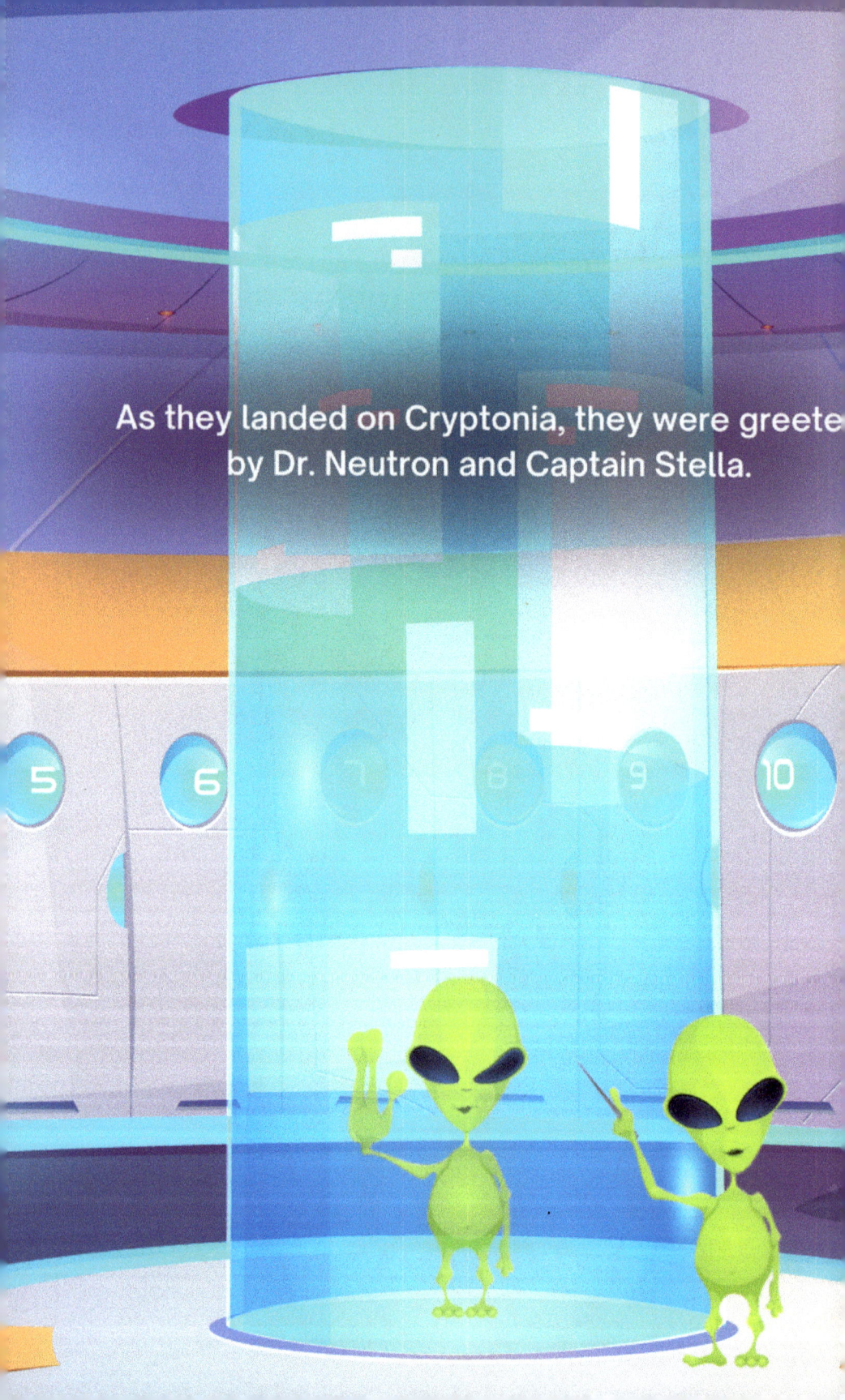

As they landed on Cryptonia, they were greeted by Dr. Neutron and Captain Stella.

"Greetings ambassadors, welcome to Crytptonia." Captain Stella said warmly. " We are honored by your visit and eager to show you our technology. But first, we need to get you registered."

Dr. Neutron, an expert in new technologies, showed them how to set up their digital wallets so that they could use it while on Cryptonia.

"Think of your new wallet like a super-secure digital vault," he explained enthusiastically. "Protect your passwords and seed phrases because it keeps your cryptocurrency safe from any sneaky space pirates."

Excited to test her new digital wallet, Rila decided to go sky surfing, a popular activity on Cryptonia. Blip, an expert sky surfer, offered her a session. He showed her how to use cryptocurrency for transactions.

"Just scan this code, and you're set to ride the winds!" Blip instructed. Rila scanned the code, and in seconds, the transaction was complete. "This is so easy and fast!" she exclaimed. "It's how we pay for things here on Cryptonia!" Blip said smiling "Now let's hit the air!"

Next, Zeno wanted to explore the nearby lake and go fishing. Captain Stella said, "Let's get you set up with a fishing license in your wallet. If a Cryptonian Ranger asks you to show it, you can pull it up digitally and prove ownership via our blockchain."

Zeno easily purchased his fishing license, verified it in his wallet and a few clicks later they were off to enjoy fun in the Cryptonian sun.

After mastering the basics of digital wallets, the crew of the Starblazer decided to explore Cryptonia's shopping district. Commander Orion was eager to buy some souvenirs for their return home. He used his digital wallet for the purchase.

"Just a quick scan," he smiled, flashing his device at the payment terminal. It was easy to use blockchain technology for everyday transactions. The crew marveled at how simple shopping could be without the need for physical money.

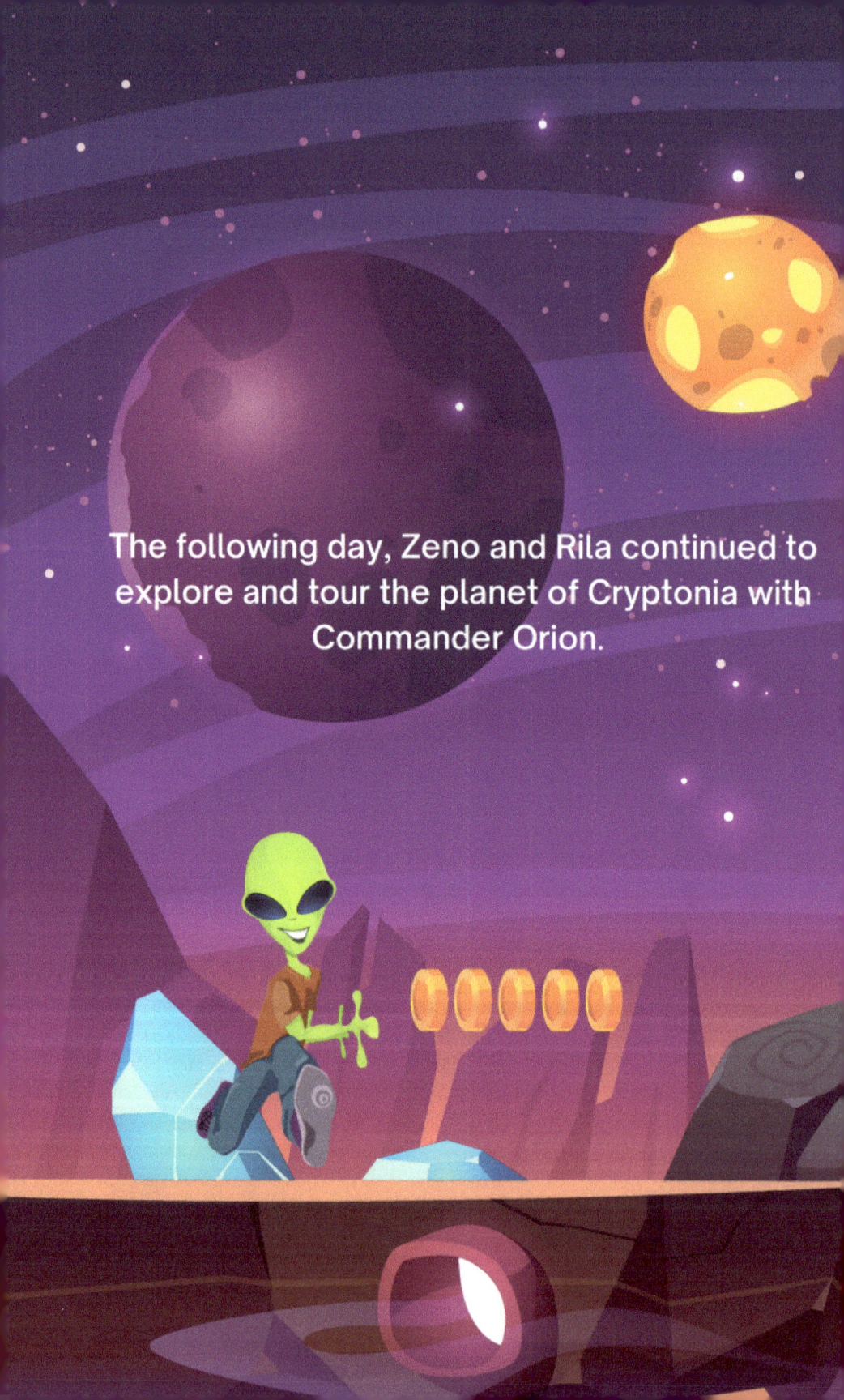

The following day, Zeno and Rila continued to explore and tour the planet of Cryptonia with Commander Orion.

They were learning much about decentralized finance as they ventured across the planet, and participated in activities like the Coinathon Space Race, and UFO flight tours.

They observed how cryptocurrency was maintained throughout the planet by a network of computers called Nodes. "It's like having a galaxy-wide team of accountants," Captain Stella explained with a smile. "Everyone helps keep the ledger accurate without a central bank."

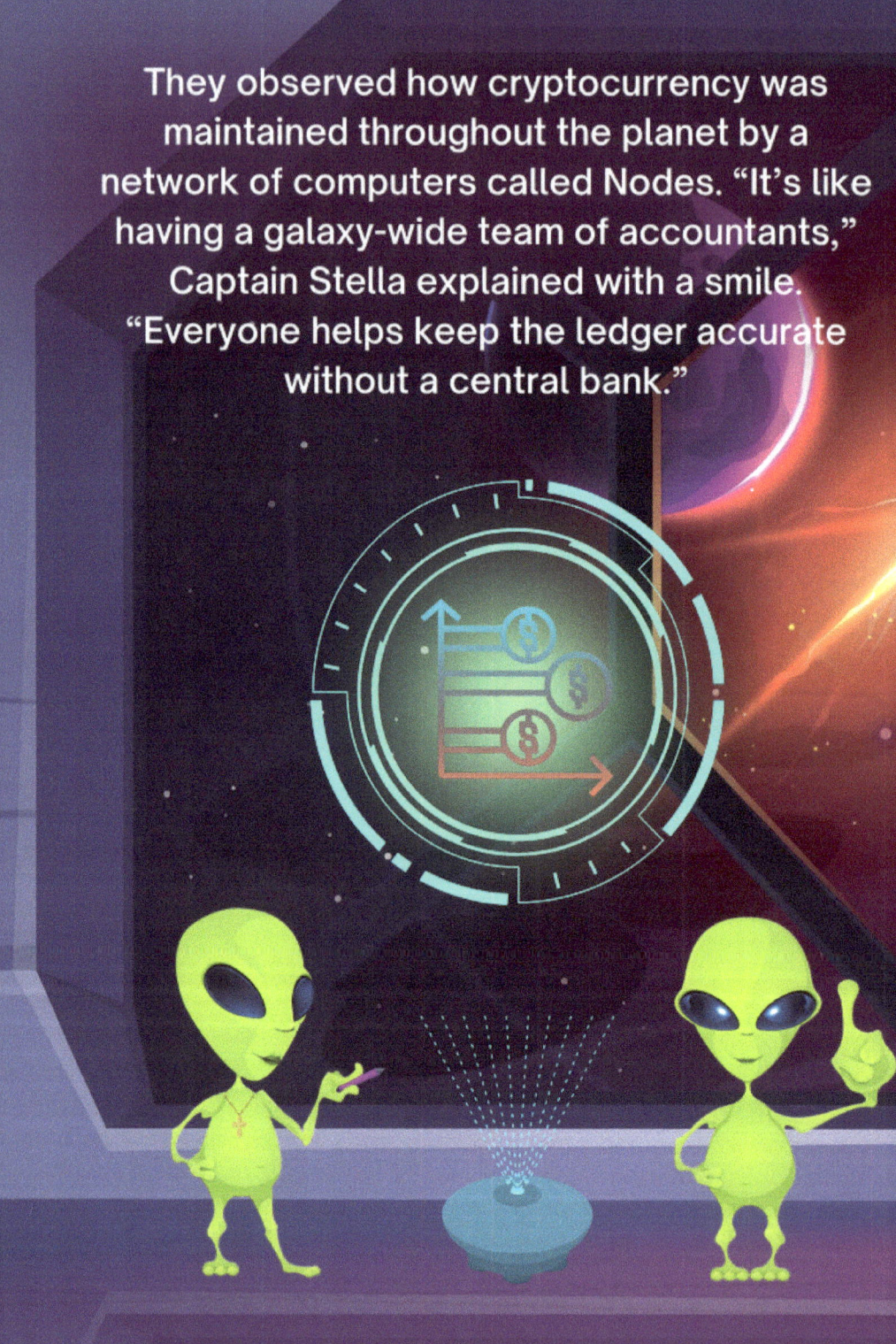

Dr. Neutron showed them a simulation, showing how multiple nodes across the network must agree, or reach consensus, for the transaction to be validated. "This consensus process is crucial. It makes our transactions not only secure but also makes it nearly impossible to alter any information retroactively," he explained. The crew nodded, intrigued by the security features.

During their adventures, the Starblazer crew also noticed that the costs for activities varied based on popularity and time.

When a famous Cryptonian DJ was announced to play at the music festival, the price of a festival ticket rose due to high demand. "This is how the value of cryptocurrency can change too!" Captain Stella explained to the crew. "It's all about supply and demand."

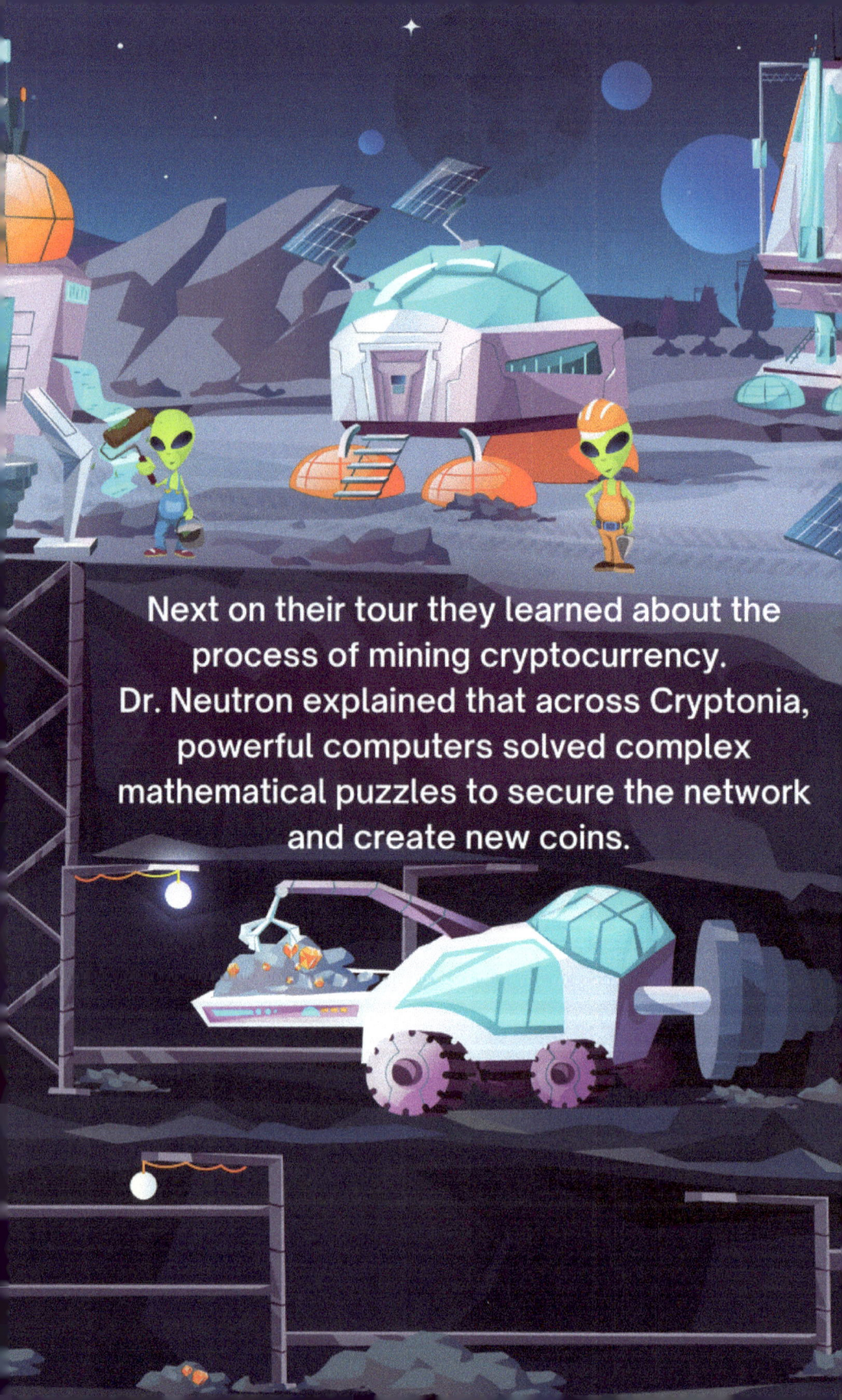

Next on their tour they learned about the process of mining cryptocurrency.
Dr. Neutron explained that across Cryptonia, powerful computers solved complex mathematical puzzles to secure the network and create new coins.

"Imagine a cosmic treasure hunt, where solving puzzles rewards you with digital gold!"
Dr. Neutron said.

All of a sudden an alarm sounded. There was a virtual attack by space pirates, attempting to disrupt the planet with fake transactions.

Captain Stella quickly addressed the threat, "It's OK. Remember, our blockchain works by validating new blocks through consensus so all of our computer Nodes have to agree and have the same copy of records. If the new record isn't correct, the block is rejected."

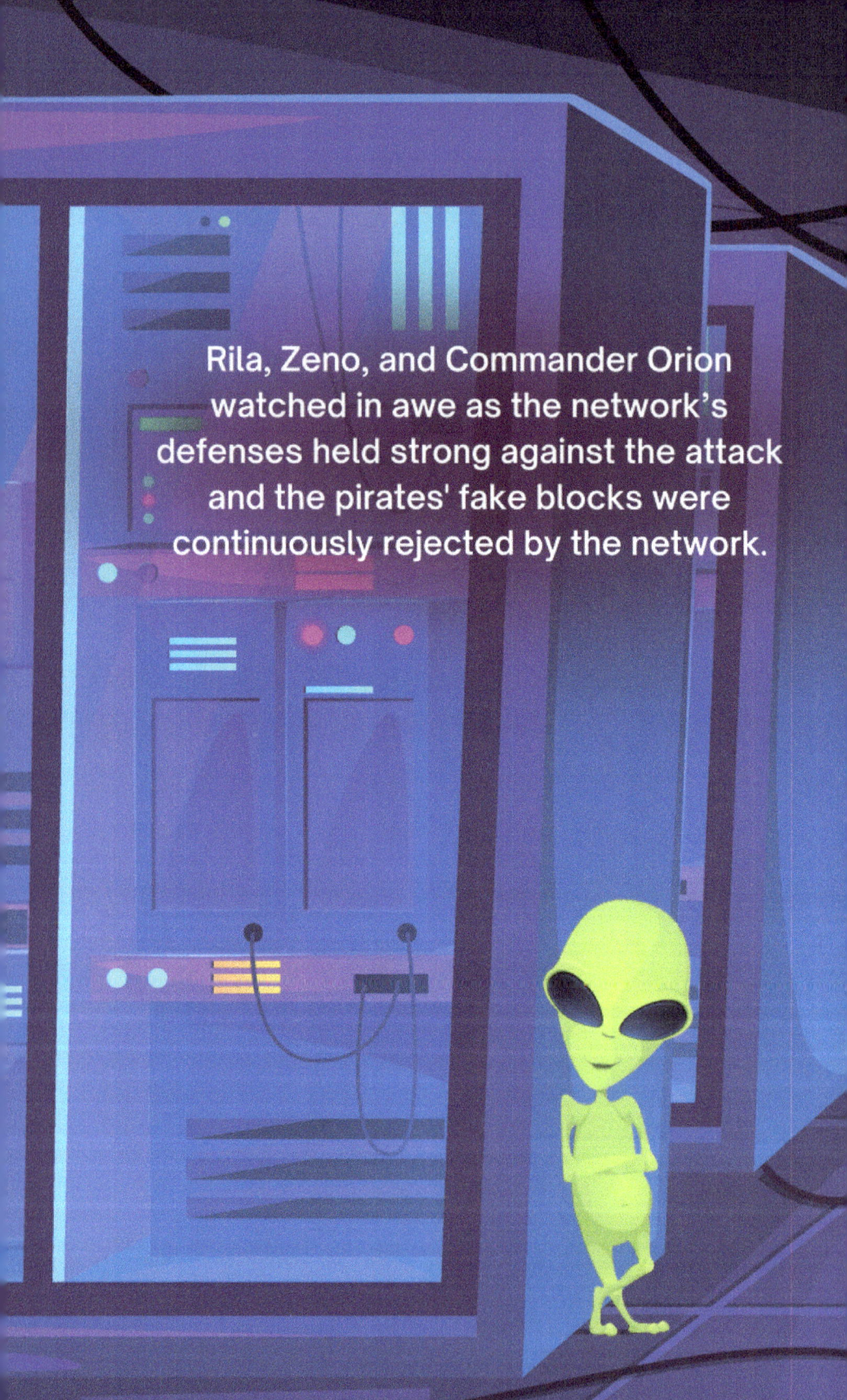

Rila, Zeno, and Commander Orion watched in awe as the network's defenses held strong against the attack and the pirates' fake blocks were continuously rejected by the network.

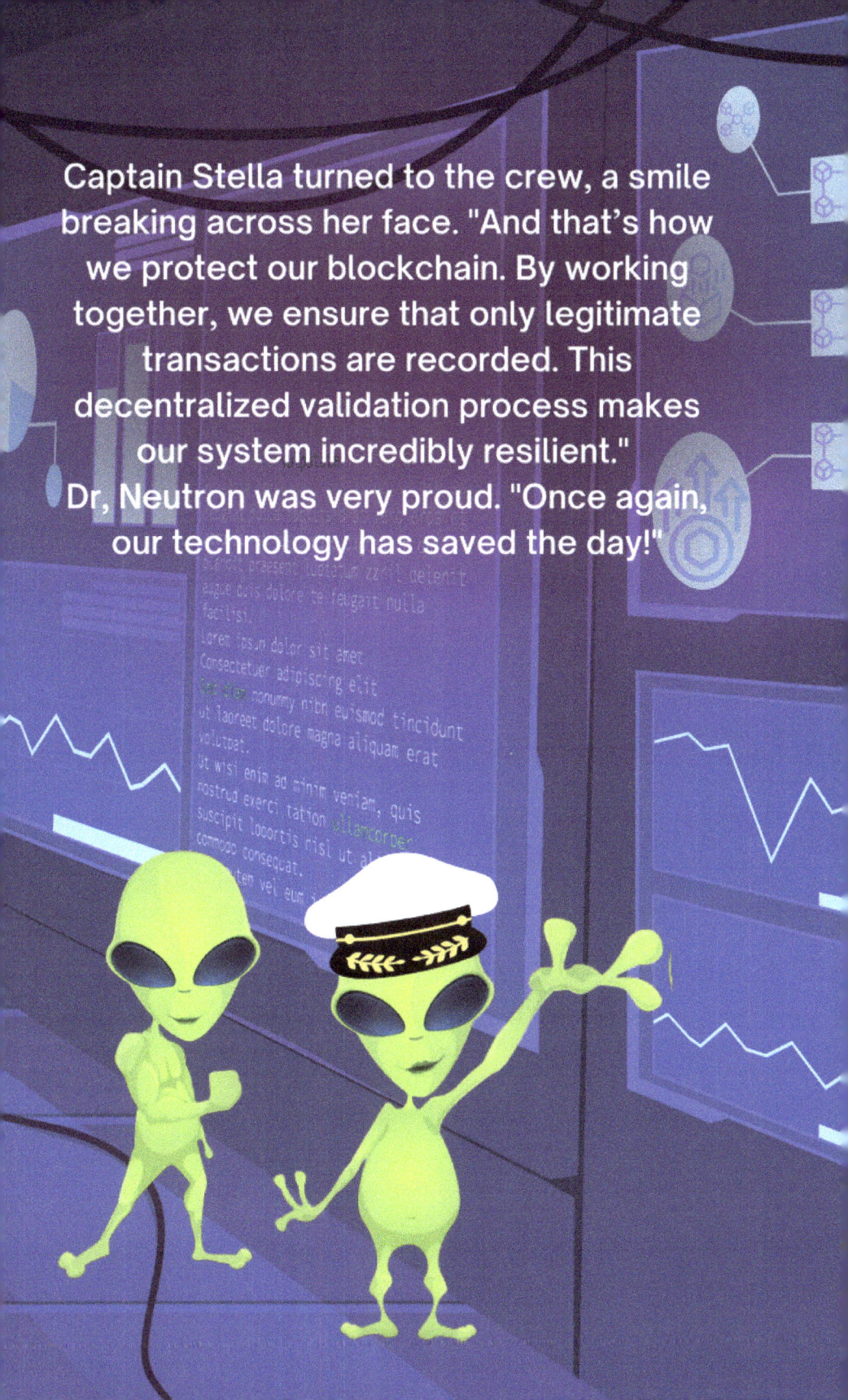

Captain Stella turned to the crew, a smile breaking across her face. "And that's how we protect our blockchain. By working together, we ensure that only legitimate transactions are recorded. This decentralized validation process makes our system incredibly resilient."
Dr, Neutron was very proud. "Once again, our technology has saved the day!"

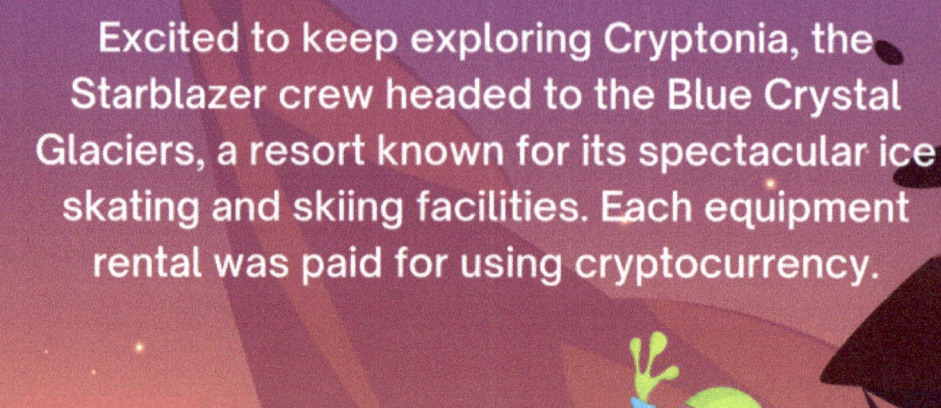

Excited to keep exploring Cryptonia, the Starblazer crew headed to the Blue Crystal Glaciers, a resort known for its spectacular ice skating and skiing facilities. Each equipment rental was paid for using cryptocurrency.

"I'm thankful that we don't need to exchange any physical currency." Captain Stella pointed out. "Our payments are direct and digital, making it incredibly convenient,"

The crew spent the day gliding over red ice and soaring over floating rock slopes, enjoying the thrill of Cryptonian sports.

Later that week, the crew visited Cryptonia's renowned Innovation Lab. Dr. Neutron used a holographic model to explain how cryptocurrency transactions are stored.

"Each transaction is encrypted and added to a block," he demonstrated. "Once filled, the block is linked to the previous one, forming a chain. This is what we call the blockchain."

On their last evening, as the fifth moon of Cryptonia rose in the sky, the crew gathered to say goodbye. "Can you believe it's time to leave already?" Zeno said with a sigh. "I know, it feels like we just arrived," Rila responded. "But think about all the incredible experiences we're taking back with us."

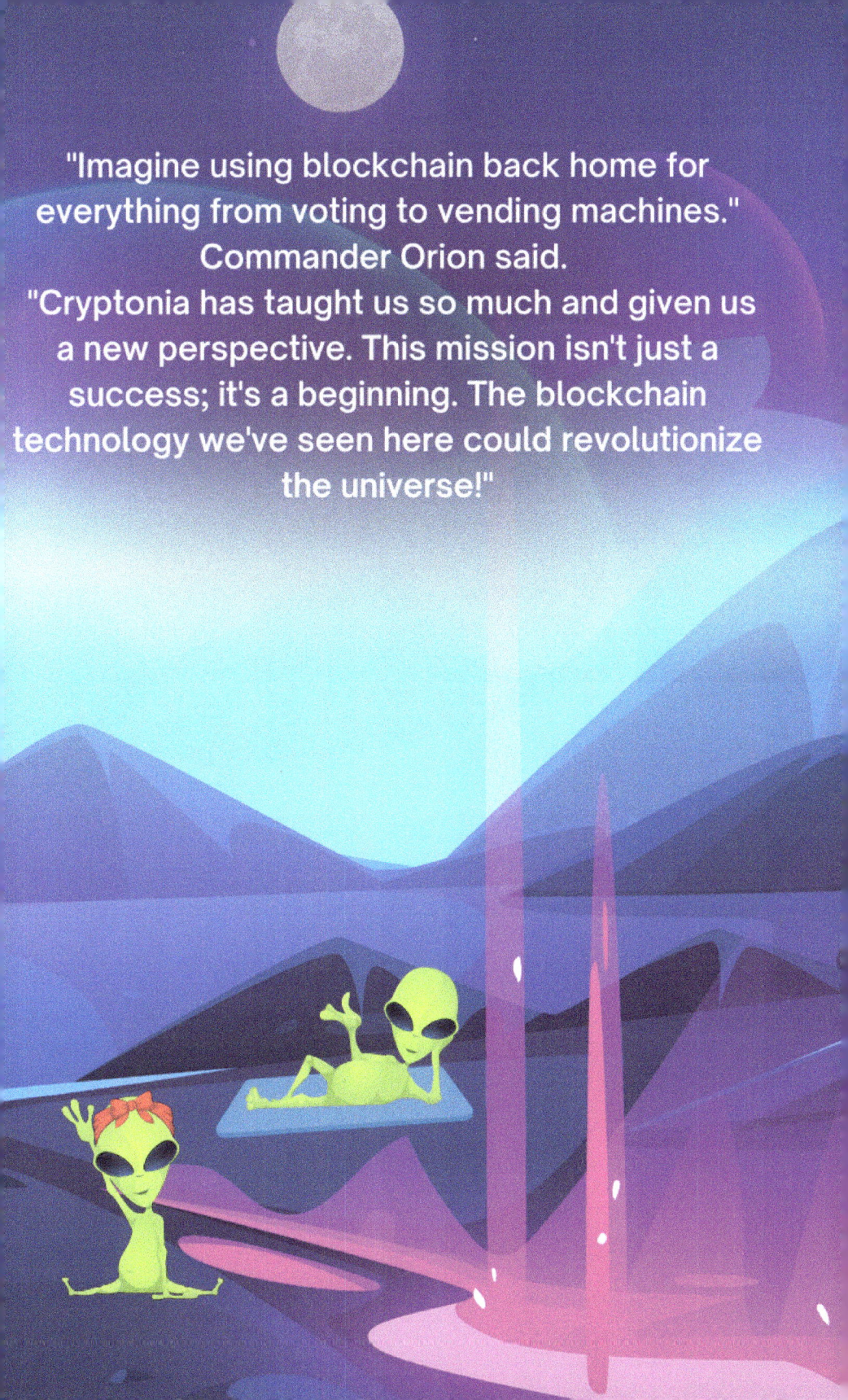

"Imagine using blockchain back home for everything from voting to vending machines." Commander Orion said.
"Cryptonia has taught us so much and given us a new perspective. This mission isn't just a success; it's a beginning. The blockchain technology we've seen here could revolutionize the universe!"

As the Starblazer lifted off, leaving the glittering lights of Cryptonia behind, the crew looked out the windows, their hearts full of memories and minds buzzing with possibilities. "We'll carry these lessons with us across the stars!" Zeno shouted out.

With that, the Starblazer zoomed off into the galaxy, its crew more ready than ever to explore the endless uses of cryptocurrency throughout the galaxy.

What is Cryptocurrency?

Cryptocurrency is a special type of digital money that you can use to buy things and pay for services. Unlike the coins and paper money you might use every day, cryptocurrencies are entirely digital, which means you can't hold them in your hand. Instead, you keep them in a digital wallet on your computer, tablet, or phone.

Here's a simple way to understand cryptocurrency:

Digital Wallets: Imagine having a super-secure vault on your device where you keep your digital money. This is your digital wallet. Just like you have a password for your email, your digital wallet has special codes called passwords and seed phrases that keep your cryptocurrency safe.

Transactions: When you want to buy something or pay someone with cryptocurrency, you don't hand over cash. Instead, you use your digital wallet to send the money over the internet. It's as easy as scanning a code or clicking a button, and the transaction happens instantly.

Blockchain: All cryptocurrency transactions are recorded on a huge digital ledger called the blockchain. Think of the blockchain as a giant book that everyone can see. Every time you send or receive cryptocurrency, a new entry is made in this book. What makes the blockchain special is that it's maintained by many computers all around the world, not just one central place. This makes it very secure and trustworthy.

Mining: New cryptocurrency is created through a process called mining. Powerful computers solve complex puzzles to add new entries to the blockchain and earn new coins as a reward.

Security: Cryptocurrency is very secure because it uses special technology to protect it. Every transaction is checked and agreed upon by many computers before it's added to the blockchain. This process, called consensus, ensures that all transactions are accurate and can't be easily changed or faked.

Supply and Demand: The value of cryptocurrency can change based on how many people want to use it. If lots of people want to buy a particular cryptocurrency, its value goes up. If fewer people want it, the value goes down. It's similar to how prices work in the real world.

Cryptocurrency is becoming more popular around the world. People use it to buy things online, send money to friends and family, and even invest for the future. Businesses are starting to accept cryptocurrency as payment, and more and more people are discovering how easy and secure it is to use. As technology continues to improve, the potential for cryptocurrency to change the way we think about money and transactions is enormous. It offers a new way to handle money that is fast, secure, and accessible to everyone.

Pixel Perfect Pets

UNIT
4

In the vibrant metaverse of Bitville, there was a special Pet Adoption Center. This center was not like any other adoption center; it was entirely digital, and all the pets were virtual.

One day, Paige, a curious and kind-hearted 5th grader, logged in to Bitville and visited the Pet Adoption Center.

She was greeted by Dr. Code, a virtual pet expert who explained how the center worked. "Here in Bitville, we use smart contracts to manage the adoption process," Dr. Code said. "Smart contracts are like digital agreements that automatically execute when certain conditions are met."

Paige was fascinated.
She listened intently as Dr. Code explained, "each virtual pet has its own smart contract, which contains information about the pet's characteristics, care requirements, and adoption fees. When someone has decided to adopt a pet, the smart contract will handle the transfer of information".

After learning about how easy the smart contracts would make the adoption process, Paige was eager to adopt a virtual pet of her own. She scrolled through the digital pets. DataDuckling and CryptoStinker flashed their best smiles. Web3Whiskers turned on the purrfect charm. And MetaRat looked like lots of fun.
But then, she saw him, the perfect pet for her. Paige found a cute virtual puppy named Pixel.

She clicked on Pixel's profile and read about his playful nature and love for adventures. Pixel was described as a curious puppy who loved exploring new virtual worlds and meeting new friends. His favorite activities included chasing virtual squirrels, fetching digital bones, and learning new tricks. Paige scrolled further and discovered Pixel had a special talent! He could perform a perfect backflip, a trick he had mastered after hours of practice. She couldn't wait to see Pixel's backflip.

Paige knew Pixel would be the perfect companion for fun adventures in Bitville.
She clicked the "Adopt Now" button, and Pixel's smart contract was started.
The smart contract automatically transferred ownership of Pixel to Paige and deducted the adoption fee from her virtual wallet.

Pixel and Paige were a great pair. She made sure to log in and take care of Pixel every day. When she logged in, Paige would first check Pixel's virtual health and happiness levels. She would then take him on walks around Bitville, where they would explore different digital lands and meet other virtual pets. She also made sure Pixel had plenty of virtual toys and treats to keep him entertained and happy.

Pixel loved spending time with Paige and looked forward to their daily adventures in Bitville.
One day Paige received an event invitation from the adoption center about their virtual pet show, the Pet Palooza.
"Pixel is the perfect pup for this, I bet he could win the contest!" She said eagerly as she signed them up.

Excitedly, Paige started training Pixel
for the Pet Show.
She taught him more tricks to go with
his backflip, groomed his virtual fur,
and prepared him for the big day.
After all, the Pet Palooza was a grand
event where pets from all over Bitville
showed their talents and skills.

On the day of the show, Paige and Pixel arrived at the virtual venue. Judge Byte welcomed them and explained how smart contracts were used to manage the show. Each pet's performance was recorded on the blockchain, ensuring fairness and transparency in the judging process.

Pixel performed brilliantly, showcasing his tricks and winning the hearts of the audience with a perfect backflip. The judges agreed, Pixel was the winner! Paige was so proud of Pixel!

As they left the Pet Show, before she logged off, Paige e-hugged Pixel and whispered, "Pixel, you're not just a virtual pet; you're a part of my heart, and I'm grateful we found each other. Thank you for being my companion."

SMART CONTRACTS EXPLAINED

Have you ever made a pinky promise with your friend?

A smart contract is like a super-powered pinky promise that can't be broken!

It's a set of digital rules or agreements that live on the internet, written in code, that automatically execute certain actions when specific conditions are met.

They work without any human involvement once they are deployed on a blockchain network.

In the story, the Virtual Pet Adoption Center used smart contracts to handle the pet adoptions. Each virtual pet had its own unique smart contract containing details about the pet, like its characteristics, care requirements, and adoption fees.

When Paige adopted Pixel the puppy, Pixel's smart contract did three very important tasks, all by itself!

💙 It gave Paige official ownership of Pixel, and provided all of Pixel's information to her.
💙 It took the adoption fee from Paige's virtual wallet to pay for adopting Pixel.
💙 It officially recorded Lily as Pixel's new owner on the blockchain ledger.

Pretty cool, right? The smart contract made sure everything happened correctly, without any human mistakes.

Smart contracts also helped at the Virtual Pet Show. The judges recorded each pet's performance on the blockchain fairly and transparently. This way, the judging process remained secure and tamper-proof, and nobody could cheat the scores.

Smart contracts are awesome because they work automatically, only when their rules are met. They're like robot assistants that never sleep and always follow instructions perfectly! This makes things super secure, efficient and reliable.

So next time you and your friend want to do something like trade a cool gaming character, imagine setting up a smart contract to do it for you! You could agree that if you trade your rare character for their special one, the smart contract would make sure the trade happens automatically. This way, both of you can trust that the trade will be fair and square, just like a pinky promise.

www.ingramcontent.com/pod-product-compliance
Lightning Source LLC
Chambersburg PA
CBHW051216120626
46547CB00013B/1385